TOM Y. BAKER
THE FINANCIAL FOUNDATIONS
BUILDING A STRONG PERSONAL ECONOMY
by Dropped Out Traders (DOT)

The Financial Foundations

Building a Strong Personal Economy

Tom Y. Baker

Copyright

THE FINANCIAL FOUNDATIONS

BUILDING A STRONG PERSONAL ECONOMY

Copyright © Dropped Out Traders (DOT)

The transmission, duplication, or reproduction of any of the following work, including any specific information, will be considered illegal, irrespective of whether it is done electronically or in print. This extends to creating a secondary or tertiary copy of the work or a recorded copy and is only allowed with express written consent from the publisher.

The information provided in the following book is broadly considered to be a truthful and accurate account of facts. As such, any inattention, use, or misuse of the information in question by the reader will render any resulting actions solely under their purview. There are no scenarios in which the publisher or the original author of this work can be in any fashion deemed liable for any hardship or damages that may befall them after undertaking the information described herein.

Furthermore, the following book is produced to provide information that is as accurate and as reliable as possible, to the best of the publisher and the original author's knowledge. Professionals should be consulted by the reader as needed prior to undertaking any of the actions endorsed herein.

Additionally, the information in the following book is intended only for informational purposes and should thus be thought of as universal. As befitting its nature, it is presented without assurance regarding its prolonged validity or interim quality. Trademarks that are mentioned are done without written consent and can in no way be considered an endorsement from the trademark holder.

All additional rights reserved.

Copyright © Dropped Out Traders (DOT)

Table of Contents

Chapter 1 Money 101: The Fundamentals of Personal Finance.- 3 -

Chapter 2 The Art of Income and Expense Management .... - 8 -

Chapter 3 Crafting a Budget That Works for You .... - 15 -

Chapter 4 Growing Your Pots .... - 21 -

Chapter 5 The ABCs of Credit and Debt .... - 27 -

Chapter 6 Protecting What Matters Most: Insurance............. - 38 -

Chapter 7 Tax Time: Understanding Your Obligations and Opportunities .... - 44 -

Chapter 8 The Financial Markets: Understanding How They Work .... - 50 -

Chapter 9 The Stock Market: Investing in Companies and Their Growth .... - 58 -

Chapter 10 Mutual Funds: Investing in a Diversified Portfolio- 66 -

Chapter 11 The Bond Market: Investing in Debt Securities .. - 74 -

Chapter 12 Diversification: The Key to Long-Term Investing Success .... - 78 -

Chapter 13 Risk and Reward: Understanding the Trade-Offs of Investing.. - 83 -

Chapter 14 Financial Advisors: How They Can Help You Achieve Your Goals .... - 86 -

Chapter 15 The Real Estate Game: Investing in Property ..... - 91 -

Chapter 16 Precious Metals: Investing in Gold and Other Commodities.. - 98 -

Chapter 17 Cryptocurrency: The Future of Money? .... - 101 -

Chapter 18 The Power of Compound Interest: Understanding Retirement Accounts .... - 108 -

Chapter 19 Inflation: Understanding Its Impact on Your Money.- 111 -

Chapter 20 Emergency Funds: Protecting Yourself from Financial Shock .... - 116 -

Chapter 21 Planning for Your Golden Years: Retirement Strategies .... - 119 -

Chapter 22 Financial Legacy: How to Leave a Positive Impact on Future Generations .... - 123 -

Empowering Yourself with Financial Freedom .... - 127 -

A Favor .... - 129 -

All Our Books .... - 130 -

The Financial Foundations

The Power of Financial Knowledge

Welcome to "The Financial Foundations: Building a Strong Personal Economy." This book is your guide to mastering the basics of personal finance and building a strong financial foundation for yourself and your loved ones.

In today's world, financial literacy is more important than ever. With a rapidly changing economy and a plethora of financial products and services at our fingertips, it's crucial that we understand the basics of money and how to manage it effectively.

But personal finance isn't just about numbers and budgets. It is about taking control of your financial future and achieving your goals. It's about feeling confident and secure in your financial decisions, and finding peace of mind in an uncertain world.

With this book, you will learn the fundamentals of personal finance, from income and expense management to budgeting, saving, and investing. You will also explore more advanced topics, such as credit and debt, insurance, real estate investing, precious metals, and cryptocurrency.

But this book isn't just about the mechanics of money. It is also about the mindset and behaviors that are essential for financial success. Such as the power of compound interest and the importance of diversification in investing.

As you read, you may find yourself asking some soul-searching questions: What are my financial goals and how can I achieve them? How can I protect myself and my loved ones from financial risk? What is my relationship with money and how can I improve it?

By the end of this book, you will have the knowledge, skills, and confidence to take control of your financial future and build a strong personal economy. So let's get started on your journey to financial freedom.

Chapter 1

Money 101: The Fundamentals of Personal Finance

Personal finance is a crucial aspect of managing one's money and achieving financial success. It involves understanding and taking control of one's financial situation, setting financial goals, and creating a plan to achieve them. There are several key areas that are included in personal finance, including budgeting, saving, investing, and planning for future expenses. In short - BSIP

B-S-I-P

Budgeting is an essential part of personal finance. It involves creating a plan for how to spend and save money each month. This can include setting aside money for bills, savings, and other expenses. By creating and sticking to a budget, individuals can avoid overspending and ensure that they have enough money to meet their financial goals.

Saving is another important aspect of personal finance. It involves setting aside money each month to build up a financial cushion for unexpected expenses or to save for the future. This can include saving for a down payment on a house, planning for retirement, or setting aside money for future expenses such as education or healthcare. By saving regularly, individuals can build up a financial safety net and be prepared for any unexpected expenses that may arise.

Investing is another key aspect of personal finance. It involves putting money into assets such as stocks, bonds, or real estate in order to grow wealth over time. This can be a great way to build wealth and achieve financial success, but it also involves taking on some level of risk. Therefore, it is important to carefully research and understand the risks and potential rewards of different investment options before making a decision.

Lastly, personal finance also involves planning for future expenses. This can include creating a plan for how to pay for college, plan for retirement, or save for a big purchase. By planning ahead and setting aside money each month, individuals can be better prepared for these future expenses and avoid financial stress.

By understanding the fundamentals of personal finance and making informed decisions, individuals can take control of their financial situation and work towards achieving their financial goals. By setting financial goals, creating a budget, saving regularly, investing wisely, and planning for the future, individuals can take the first steps towards achieving financial stability and success.

Debts and Risks

One thing that is often overlooked is personal finance also involves managing and reducing debt. This can include paying off credit card balances, student loans, or other forms of debt in a timely and responsible manner. By reducing debt, individuals can improve their credit score and free up more money to save and invest for the future.

Another important aspect of personal finance is protecting against financial risks. This can include purchasing insurance to protect against potential losses, such as health insurance to protect against the cost of medical care, or life insurance to provide financial support for loved ones in the event of the policyholder's death. By taking steps to protect against financial risks, individuals can help to secure their financial future and protect their loved ones.

A good personal finance plan involves setting financial goals and creating a plan to achieve them. This can include saving for a down payment on a house, planning for retirement, or setting aside money for future expenses such as education or healthcare. A good personal finance plan also involves regularly reviewing and adjusting the plan to ensure that it is still on track to meet the individual's financial goals.

On the other hand, a bad personal finance plan can involve overspending, not saving enough for the future, or taking on too much debt. This can lead to financial instability and make it difficult to achieve financial goals. For example, if an individual spends all of their income each month without setting aside any money for savings, they may struggle to afford unexpected expenses or save for the future.

A Complex Goal

Personal finance is, without a doubt, a complex and important aspect of managing one's money and achieving financial success. It involves budgeting, saving, investing, planning for the future, reducing debt, and protecting against financial risks. By understanding and carefully managing these areas, individuals can take control of their financial situation and work towards achieving their financial goals.

Chapter 2

The Art of Income and Expense Management

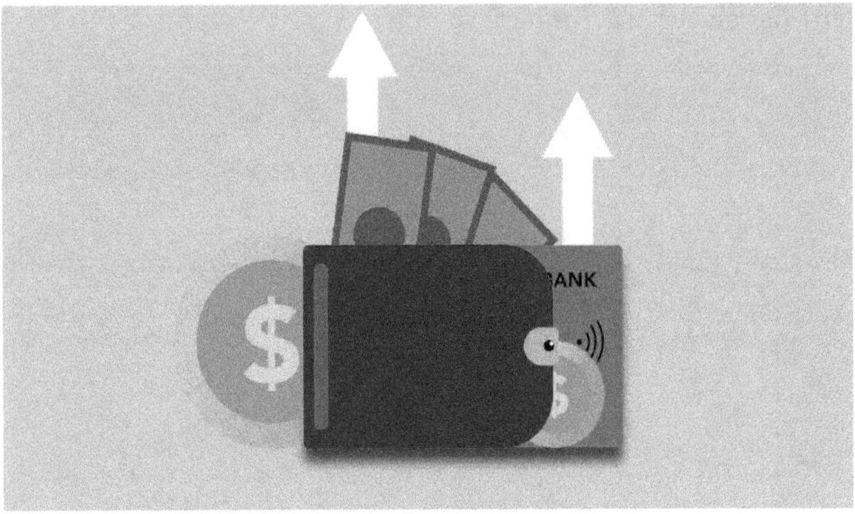

It is important to manage income and expenses because doing so can help individuals and businesses to achieve their financial goals and maintain financial stability. By carefully managing income and expenses, individuals and businesses can ensure that they have enough money to pay for their expenses and save for the future.

One reason why it is important to manage income and expenses is to avoid overspending. If an individual or a business spends more money than they earn, they can end up in financial trouble. This can lead to high levels of debt, which can be difficult to repay and can damage an individual's or a business's credit score. By carefully managing income and expenses, individuals and businesses can avoid overspending and ensure that they are able to pay their bills and meet their financial obligations.

Another reason why it is important to manage income and expenses is to save for the future. By setting aside money each month for savings, individuals and businesses can build up a financial cushion to help them weather unexpected expenses or plan for future expenses such as education or retirement. By carefully managing income and expenses, individuals and businesses can ensure that they have enough money to save for the future and achieve their financial goals.

Income vs Expenses

Income is the money that an individual or a business receives in exchange for goods or services. This can include wages and salaries, interest and dividends from investments, and profits from a business. Income is an important part of personal finance because it provides the money that individuals and businesses need to pay for their expenses and achieve their financial goals.

Expenses, on the other hand, are the money that an individual or a business spends in order to operate and maintain their lifestyle or business. This can include expenses such as rent or mortgage payments, utilities, food, clothing, and transportation. Expenses are an important part of personal finance because they represent the money that individuals and businesses need to spend in order to maintain their standard of living or operate their business.

The Angels

One example of income is a salary. If an individual works at a job, they may receive a salary in exchange for their labor. This salary provides the money that the individual can use to pay for their expenses and achieve their financial goals.

Another example of income is interest and dividends from investments. If an individual invests their money in stocks, bonds, or other assets, they may receive interest and dividends as a return on their investment. This income provides the individual with additional money that they can use to pay for their expenses or save for the future.

The Devils

One example of an expense is rent or a mortgage payment. If an individual owns a home, they will need to pay a monthly rent or mortgage payment in order to maintain ownership of the property. This expense represents the money that the individual needs to spend in order to have a place to live.

Another example of an expense is food. In order to maintain their health and well-being, individuals need to purchase and consume food on a regular basis. This can represent a significant expense, particularly if an individual chooses to eat out or purchase high-quality food.

In conclusion, income is the money that an individual or a business receives in exchange for goods or services, while expenses are the money that an individual or a business spends in order to maintain their standard of living or operate their business. Income provides the funds that individuals and businesses need to pay for their expenses and achieve their financial goals, while expenses represent the money that must be spent in order to maintain their lifestyle or business operations.

Income-Expense Ratio

The income-expense ratio is a measure of how much of a person's income is going toward expenses. This ratio is calculated using the formula: income-expense ratio = total monthly expenses / total monthly income. To use this formula, a person must add up all of their monthly expenses and divide that number by their total monthly income. The result will be a decimal number that can be multiplied by 100 to express the ratio as a percentage.

For example, if a person's total monthly expenses are $2,000 and their total monthly income is $5,000, their income-expense ratio would be 0.4, or 40%. This means that 40% of their income is going toward expenses.

It is important to learn about the income-expense ratio because it is a useful tool for managing your personal finances. The income-expense ratio helps you understand how much of your income is going toward expenses, which can be helpful in making decisions about how to allocate your money and create a budget.

Having a good understanding of your income-expense ratio can also help you identify areas where you may be able to cut back on expenses or save more money. For example, if you find that a large portion of your income is going toward credit card payments or other high-interest debt, you may want to consider ways to reduce these expenses in order to improve your financial situation.

Additionally, the income-expense ratio can be a useful measure of your financial health. If your income-expense ratio is high (meaning a large portion of your income is going toward expenses), it may be a sign that you are living beyond your means and could be at risk for financial difficulties. On the other hand, if your income-expense ratio is low, it may indicate that you are on track with your finances and have some flexibility in your budget.

Saving Rate

On top of above, there is another formula that can help individuals manage their income and expenses, which is none other than Saving Rate.

The savings rate is a measure of how much of your income you save each month. It is calculated by dividing your total savings by your total income. For example, if you save $500 per month and earn $3,000 per month, your savings rate would be 16.67%.

The savings rate is an important calculation because it helps you understand how much money you are putting away for the future and whether you are on track to reach your savings goals. A high savings rate is generally considered to be a sign of good financial health, as it means that you are able to save a significant portion of your income and build a nest egg for the future.

In addition to helping you understand your current savings habits, the savings rate can also be a useful tool for setting savings goals. For example, if you have a low savings rate, you may want to consider ways to increase your savings in order to improve your financial situation. This could involve cutting back on expenses, increasing your income, or finding ways to save more money.

Chapter 3

Crafting a Budget That Works for You

A Good Budget

A good budget is a financial plan that helps you manage your income and expenses in a way that supports your financial goals. A good budget should be based on your individual circumstances and goals, and it should be realistic and achievable.

There are several key elements that make up a good budget. First, a good budget should include a clear picture of your current financial situation, including your income, expenses, assets, and liabilities. This will help you understand your starting point and identify areas where you may be able to make changes or improvements.

Second, a good budget should include specific savings goals. This could include saving for a down payment on a house, building an emergency fund, or saving for retirement. Having specific savings goals will help you prioritize your spending and make sure you are putting money aside for the things that are most important to you.

Third, a good budget should include a plan for managing your expenses. This could involve creating a spending plan that outlines how much money you will allocate to different categories of expenses, such as housing, transportation, food, and entertainment. A good budget should also include strategies for reducing or eliminating unnecessary expenses in order to free up more money for savings.

Budgeting Framework

Crafting a good budgeting strategy involves several steps:

1. Identify your financial goals: The first step in crafting a good budgeting strategy is to identify your financial goals. This could include saving for a down payment on a house, paying off credit card debt, building an emergency fund, or saving for retirement. Having specific goals will help you prioritize your spending and

make sure you are putting money aside for the things that are most important to you.

2. Understand your current financial situation: The next step is to understand your current financial situation. This means gathering information about your income, expenses, assets, and liabilities. This will help you understand your starting point and identify areas where you may be able to make changes or improvements.

3. Create a spending plan: Once you have a clear picture of your financial goals and your current situation, you can create a spending plan. This should outline how much money you will allocate to different categories of expenses, such as housing, transportation, food, and entertainment. Your spending plan should be realistic and achievable, and it should allow for some flexibility in case your circumstances or goals change.

4. Identify ways to reduce or eliminate expenses: A good budgeting strategy should also include strategies for reducing or eliminating unnecessary expenses. This could involve cutting back on non-essential spending, negotiating lower rates for bills and services, or finding ways to save money on groceries and other household expenses.

5. Monitor and adjust your budget regularly: Finally, it's important to regularly monitor and adjust your budget as needed. This means tracking your spending and comparing it to your budget to make sure you are staying on track. If you find that you are not meeting your goals or that your circumstances have changed, you may need to make adjustments to your budget in order to stay on track.

The Common Mistakes

There are many common mistakes that people make when it comes to personal budgeting. Some examples of bad personal budgeting include not having a budget at all, creating a budget that is unrealistic or unachievable, not tracking your spending, and not adjusting your budget as needed.

One of the most common mistakes in personal budgeting is not having a budget at all. Without a budget, it's difficult to know how much money you have coming in and going out, which can lead to overspending and financial difficulties. A budget is a critical tool for managing your income and expenses, and it's important to create one that is realistic and achievable.

Another mistake in personal budgeting is creating a budget that is unrealistic or unachievable. For example, if your budget includes excessive savings goals or overly restrictive spending limits, it may be difficult or impossible to stick to. As a result, you may become frustrated or discouraged and give up on your budget altogether. It's important to create a budget that is based on your individual circumstances and goals, and that allows for some flexibility in case your situation changes.

A third mistake in personal budgeting is not tracking your spending. Without tracking your spending, it's difficult to know whether you are staying on track with your budget or if you need to make adjustments. As a result, you may find that you are overspending in certain areas or not meeting your savings goals. To avoid this mistake, it's important to regularly track your spending and compare it to your budget to make sure you are staying on track.

Finally, another common mistake in personal budgeting is not adjusting your budget as needed. Circumstances and goals can change over time, and it's important to regularly review and update your budget to make sure it is still realistic and achievable. If you don't adjust your budget, you may find that it no longer aligns with your current situation, which can lead to financial difficulties. To avoid this mistake, it's important to regularly review and update your budget to ensure that it continues to meet your needs.

Budgeting is important in our lives because it helps us manage our income and expenses in a way that supports our financial goals. A budget is a financial plan that outlines how much money you have coming in and going out, and it helps you understand where your money is going and whether you are on track to meet your savings goals. A budget is a critical tool for avoiding overspending and financial difficulties, saving money, and making informed decisions about our money.

Chapter 4

Growing Your Pots

Early Birds

One of the most important strategies for saving and investing is to start as early as possible. The earlier you start saving and investing, the more time your money has to grow and compound. This can help you build a larger nest egg over time and improve your chances of reaching your financial goals. For example, if you start saving and investing at age 25, you may have more than twice as much money saved by the time you reach retirement age compared to someone who starts at age 35.

Too old to start?

What if you are already in your thirties? Fret not, there are many strategies you can use to save more money. Some additional savings strategies include automating your savings, taking advantage of employer matching programs, using cashback rewards and discounts, and creating a side hustle.

One way to make sure you are saving consistently is to automate your savings. This could involve setting up automatic transfers from your checking account to your savings account, or enrolling in a retirement plan that automatically deducts money from your paycheck. By automating your savings, you can make sure that you are putting money aside on a regular basis without having to think about it. This can be a useful strategy for people who find it difficult to save consistently or who have a tendency to spend their money as soon as they receive it.

Many employers offer matching programs for retirement savings, which means that they will match a certain percentage of the money that you contribute to your retirement plan. For example, if your employer offers a 50% match on your 401(k) contributions, and you contribute $500 per month, your employer will also contribute $250 per month. This is free money that can help you save more for retirement, so it's important to take advantage of these programs if they are available. Employer matching programs can be a powerful way to boost your savings and grow your nest egg over time.

Another way to save money is to take advantage of cashback rewards and discounts. Many credit cards and loyalty programs offer cashback rewards or discounts on certain purchases, and these rewards can add up over time. For example, if you use a credit card that offers 1% cashback on all purchases, and you spend $1,000 per month, you will earn $10 in cashback each month. This is money that you can use to boost your savings or reduce your expenses. By using cashback rewards and discounts, you can save money on your everyday purchases and put that money towards your savings or investing goals.

Another strategy for saving more money is to create a side hustle. A side hustle is a part-time business or income- generating activity that you can do in addition to your full-time job. For example, you might start a blog, sell handmade crafts on Etsy, or offer your services as a tutor or freelancer. A side hustle can be a great way to earn extra money and boost your savings. It can also be a rewarding way to pursue your passions and interests, and it can provide you with a sense of accomplishment and fulfillment.

The Importance of Saving

Saving money is an important part of managing your finances and achieving your financial goals. There are several reasons why saving money is important, including avoiding financial difficulties, reaching your financial goals, preparing for the future, and reducing stress and anxiety.

One of the most important reasons to save money is to avoid financial difficulties. By saving money, you can build an emergency fund that you can use to cover unexpected expenses, such as medical bills, car repairs, or lost income. This can help you avoid having to borrow money or rely on credit cards to pay for unexpected expenses, which can put you at risk of debt and financial problems. Having an emergency fund can give you peace of mind and help you feel more financially secure.

Another important reason to save money is to reach your financial goals. By setting specific savings goals, such as saving for a down payment on a house or building an emergency fund, you can make sure that you are putting money aside for the things that are most important to you. Saving money can help you achieve your financial goals and improve your financial security. For example, if you want to save for a down payment on a house, you can set a savings goal and create a plan for achieving that goal, such as saving a certain amount of money each month or increasing your income.

Saving money is also important for preparing for the future. This could include saving for retirement, saving for your children's education, or saving for a major purchase, such as a car or a vacation. By saving money, you can make sure that you have the financial resources you need to live the life you want in the future. For example, if you want to retire comfortably, you may need to save a significant amount of money over the course of your career in order to have enough money to live on in retirement.

Finally, saving money can also help reduce stress and anxiety. When you have a solid savings plan in place, you can feel more confident and secure about your financial future. This can reduce stress and anxiety and help you live a happier and more fulfilling life. For example, if you have a well-funded emergency fund, you can feel more confident and secure knowing that you have the financial resources to cover unexpected expenses. This can help you feel more relaxed and in control of your finances, which can improve your overall well-being.

By making saving a priority and developing a plan for achieving your savings goals, you can improve your financial situation and achieve your goals.

Chapter 5

The ABCs of Credit and Debt

Credit and debt are an important part of our financial lives. Credit allows us to borrow money to make purchases or investments, while debt is the amount of money we owe to lenders. In this chapter, we will explore the ABCs of credit and debt, including how credit works, the different types of credit, and strategies for managing debt.

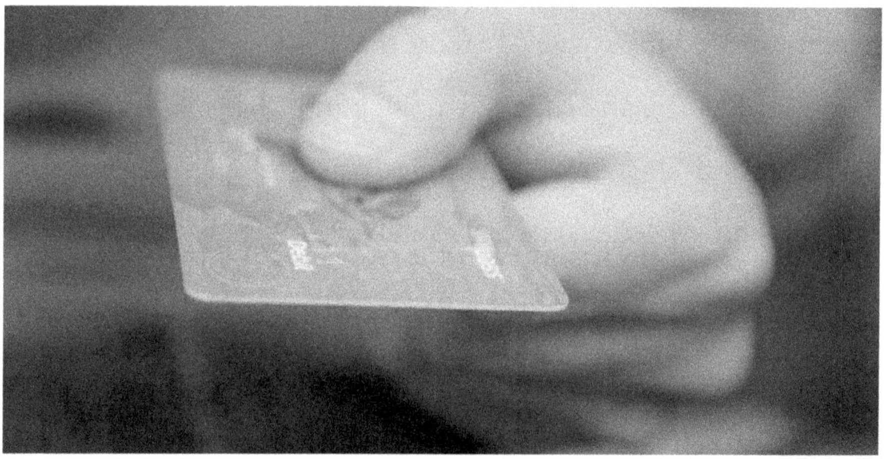

Types of Credit

Credit is a financial tool that allows us to borrow money to make purchases or investments. There are several different types of credit, including revolving credit, installment credit, open-end credit, secured credit, and unsecured credit.

Revolving credit is a type of credit that allows you to borrow money up to a certain limit, and then pay back the money you borrow, plus interest, over time. Examples of revolving credit include credit cards and home equity lines of credit (HELOCs). With revolving credit, you can borrow and repay money repeatedly, as long as you do not exceed your credit limit.

Installment credit is a type of credit that allows you to borrow a set amount of money, and then pay it back in fixed monthly payments over a set period of time. Examples of installment credit include car loans, student loans, and personal loans. With installment credit, you borrow a fixed amount of money and agree to pay it back in equal monthly payments over a set period of time.

Open-end credit is a type of credit that allows you to borrow money up to a certain limit, and then pay back the money you borrow, plus interest, over time. Unlike revolving credit, open-end credit requires you to pay off the entire balance each month, rather than carrying a balance from month to month. Examples of open-end credit include charge cards and open-end mortgages.

Secured credit is a type of credit that is backed by collateral, such as a car or a home. If you fail to make your payments, the lender can seize the collateral to cover their losses. Examples of secured credit include car loans and mortgages. With secured credit, you provide collateral to the lender as a guarantee that you will repay your debts.

Unsecured credit is a type of credit that is not backed by collateral. If you fail to make your payments, the lender cannot seize your assets to cover their losses. Examples of unsecured credit include credit cards and personal loans. With unsecured credit, you do not provide collateral to the lender, so they rely on your creditworthiness and ability to repay your debts.

Each type of credit has its own unique features and benefits. By understanding the different types of credit, you can make informed decisions about borrowing and repayment, and choose the type of credit that is right for your needs and financial situation.

Credit Score and Credit Report

A credit score is a numerical representation of your creditworthiness. It is a measure of how likely you are to repay your debts and is based on factors such as your payment history, the amount of credit you have available, and your credit utilization ratio (the amount of credit you are using compared to the amount of credit you have available). A high credit score can make it easier to qualify for credit and can help you get better terms, such as lower interest rates.

For example, if you have a credit score of 750, you may be able to qualify for a lower interest rate on a mortgage or a car loan. On the other hand, if you have a credit score of 550, you may have a harder time qualifying for credit and may have to pay a higher interest rate if you are able to get a loan.

It's important to understand your credit score and take steps to improve it if necessary. You can get a free copy of your credit score from each of the three major credit bureaus (Equifax, Experian, and TransUnion) once a year. You can also check your credit score for free on websites such as CreditKarma or CreditSesame. By regularly checking your credit score, you can monitor your creditworthiness and take steps to improve it if necessary.

Your credit score and credit report are closely related. Your credit score is based on the information in your credit report, so it's important to review your credit report regularly to make sure it is accurate and up-to-date. By understanding your credit score and credit report, you can make informed decisions about borrowing and repayment, and take steps to improve your credit score and enhance your financial situation.

Paths to Building a Good Credit Score

There are several steps you can take to build a good credit score. Here are a few tips:

Pay your bills on time: One of the most important factors in your credit score is your payment history. By paying your bills on time, you can show creditors that you are a responsible borrower and improve your credit score.

Keep your credit utilization low: Your credit utilization is the amount of credit you are using compared to the amount of credit you have available. A high credit utilization can harm your credit score, so it's important to keep your balances low and pay off as much of your credit card debt as possible.

Don't open too many credit accounts at once: Opening too many credit accounts in a short period of time can harm your credit score. If you need to open a new credit account, do it gradually and make sure you can manage the additional credit responsibly.

Check your credit report regularly: Your credit report contains information about your credit history, including your payment history and the amount of credit you have available. By checking your credit report regularly, you can identify and correct any errors that may be harming your credit score.

Building a good credit score requires careful management of your credit accounts and regular monitoring of your credit report.

Managing Debts

Managing debt is an important part of achieving your financial goals and maintaining your financial health. There are several different strategies you can use to manage your debt, including the following:

Budgeting: One of the most effective strategies for managing debt is to create a budget. A budget is a plan for how you will spend and save your money each month. By creating a budget, you can see where your money is going and identify areas where you can reduce your spending or increase your income. This can help you free up money to pay off your debts and improve your financial situation.

Debt consolidation: Another strategy for managing debt is to consolidate your debts into a single loan or credit account. This can make it easier to manage your debts and make your monthly payments, because you will only have to make one payment instead of multiple payments. Debt consolidation can also help you save money on interest, because you may be able to qualify for a lower interest rate on a consolidated loan or credit account.

Debt repayment plan: A debt repayment plan is a structured plan for paying off your debts. This can involve prioritizing your debts, such as paying off the debts with the highest interest rates first, or using the debt snowball or debt avalanche methods to pay off your debts. A debt repayment plan can help you stay organized and focused, and it can provide a roadmap for achieving your debt repayment goals.

Credit counseling: Credit counseling is a service that helps people manage their debts. Credit counselors can provide advice on budgeting, debt repayment, and credit repair. They can also help you develop a plan for paying off your debts and improving your credit score. Credit counseling can be a valuable resource for managing your debts and achieving your financial goals.

Bankruptcy: In some cases, bankruptcy may be an option for managing your debts. Bankruptcy is a legal process that allows you to discharge your debts and get a fresh financial start. There are two main types of bankruptcy: Chapter 7 and Chapter 13. Chapter 7 bankruptcy allows you to discharge most of your debts, while Chapter 13 bankruptcy allows you to reorganize your debts and repay them over time. Bankruptcy can be a last resort for managing your debts, and it can have a major impact on your credit score and your financial situation.

By budgeting, consolidating your debts, creating a debt repayment plan, seeking credit counseling, and considering bankruptcy if necessary, you can manage your debts and achieve your financial goals.

The DTI Ratio

The debt-to-income ratio (DTI) is a measure of your ability to repay your debts. It is calculated by dividing your monthly debt payments by your monthly income. For example, if you have monthly debt payments of $800 and monthly income of $2,000, your debt-to-income ratio is 40%.

Lenders use your debt-to-income ratio to evaluate your ability to repay your debts. A high debt-to-income ratio can indicate that you may have difficulty making your monthly debt payments, which can make it difficult to qualify for credit or can result in higher interest rates.

It's important to manage your debt-to-income ratio carefully, because having too much debt relative to your income can put you at risk of financial difficulties. To improve your debt-to-income ratio, you can try to increase your income, reduce your monthly debt payments, or do both. For example, you could look for ways to earn more money, such as taking on extra work or starting a side business. You could also try to reduce your monthly debt payments by refinancing your loans, consolidating your debts, or negotiating lower interest rates.

The debt-to-income ratio is an important measure of your ability to repay your debts. By managing your debt-to-income ratio carefully, you can improve your chances of qualifying for credit and getting favorable interest rates, and you can avoid financial difficulties.

Credit + Debt = Part of Your Life

Credit and debt are an important part of our financial lives for several reasons.

First, credit allows us to borrow money to make purchases or investments that we may not be able to afford with cash. For example, if you want to buy a home but don't have enough money saved up, you can use a mortgage to borrow the money you need to make the purchase. Credit can also be useful for covering unexpected expenses, such as medical bills or home repairs.

Second, credit can help us build and improve our credit score. Your credit score is a numerical representation of your creditworthiness, and it is based on factors such as your payment history and the amount of credit you have available. A high credit score can make it easier to qualify for credit and can help you get better terms, such as lower interest rates. By using credit responsibly and making your payments on time, you can build and improve your credit score over time.

Third, debt can help us finance important purchases or investments that can improve our financial situation. For example, if you take out a student loan to pay for college, you may be able to earn a higher income after graduation, which can help you repay your loan and improve your financial situation. Similarly, if you use a mortgage to buy a home, you may be able to build equity in the property, which can increase your net worth and improve your financial situation.

These are important because they allow us to borrow money to make purchases or investments, help us build and improve our credit score, and provide access to financing that can improve our financial situation. By understanding credit and debt and managing them wisely, we can improve our financial health and achieve our financial goals.

Chapter 6

Protecting What Matters Most: Insurance

Insurance is a financial product that provides protection against financial loss. It is a contract between an insurer and an insured, in which the insurer agrees to provide financial compensation in the event of a covered loss. The insured pays a premium to the insurer in exchange for this protection.

There are many different types of insurance, including life insurance, health insurance, auto insurance, and homeowners insurance. Each type of insurance provides protection against different risks and losses. For example, life insurance provides financial protection for your loved ones in the event of your death, while health insurance provides coverage for medical expenses. Auto insurance provides protection against losses resulting from car accidents, while homeowners insurance provides protection against losses to your home and personal property.

Insurance can help protect you and your loved ones from financial loss in the event of a covered loss. It can provide peace of mind and financial security, and it can help you manage the financial risks of everyday life. By purchasing insurance, you can transfer some of the financial risks you face to an insurer, who will provide financial compensation if a covered loss occurs.

Types of Insurance

There are several different types of personal insurance, including:

Life insurance: Life insurance provides financial protection for your loved ones in the event of your death. It pays out a death benefit to your beneficiaries, who can use the money to pay for expenses such as funeral costs, outstanding debts, and living expenses. There are two main types of life insurance: term life insurance, which provides coverage for a specific period of time, and whole life insurance, which provides lifelong coverage.

Health insurance: Health insurance provides coverage for medical expenses, such as doctor visits, hospital stays, and prescription drugs. Health insurance can help you pay for the costs of healthcare, which can be very expensive. There are several different types of health insurance, including employer-sponsored group plans, individual plans, and government-sponsored plans such as Medicare and Medicaid.

Auto insurance: Auto insurance provides protection against losses resulting from car accidents. It covers the costs of repairing or replacing your car, as well as the costs of medical care for you and your passengers. Auto insurance also provides liability coverage, which can help protect you if you are found to be at fault in an accident.

Homeowners insurance: Homeowners insurance provides protection against losses to your home and personal property. It covers the costs of repairing or rebuilding your home if it is damaged or destroyed, as well as the costs of replacing your personal belongings if they are stolen or damaged. Homeowners insurance also provides liability coverage, which can help protect you if someone is injured on your property.

Myth and Truth

There are several myths about insurance that are not true. Here are a few of those myths and the truths behind them:

Myth: Insurance is a waste of money because you never know if you will actually need it.

Truth: Insurance is not a waste of money because it provides protection against financial loss. If you suffer a covered loss, your insurance will provide financial compensation that can help you pay for expenses and avoid financial difficulties. While it is true that you may not always need to use your insurance, it can provide valuable protection if you do suffer a covered loss.

Myth: Insurance is too expensive, so it's not worth it.

Truth: Insurance can be an important part of your financial plan, and it can provide valuable protection against financial loss. The cost of insurance is based on a variety of factors, including the type of insurance, the amount of coverage, and the risks involved. While insurance may not be free, it can provide valuable protection that is well worth the cost.

Myth: Insurance companies are out to rip you off, so you can't trust them.

Truth: Insurance companies are regulated by state and federal laws, and they are required to act in good faith and treat their customers fairly. While it is true that some insurance companies may not always act in the best interests of their customers, the vast majority of insurance companies are reputable and trustworthy. You can research different insurance companies and compare their policies to find the one that best meets your needs.

A Hedge

Insurance is a hedging tool because it helps to protect against financial loss. A hedge is something that reduces the risk of financial loss, and insurance is a type of hedge because it provides financial compensation in the event of a covered loss.

For example, if you have health insurance and you get sick or injured, your health insurance will help to pay for your medical expenses. This can protect you from the financial burden of high medical costs, and it can help to reduce the risk of financial loss. Similarly, if you have auto insurance and you get into a car accident, your auto insurance will help to pay for the costs of repairing or replacing your car, as well as the costs of medical care for you and your passengers. This can protect you from the financial burden of car accident expenses, and it can help to reduce the risk of financial loss.

Insurance is a hedging tool because it provides financial protection against financial loss. By purchasing insurance, you can transfer some of the financial risks you face to an insurer, who will provide financial compensation if a covered loss occurs. This can help to reduce the risk of financial loss and provide financial security.

Chapter 7

Tax Time: Understanding Your Obligations and Opportunities

What is Tax?

Personal tax obligation is a crucial aspect of financial planning. As an individual, you are responsible for paying taxes on your income and other taxable income. This means that you must understand your tax obligations and ensure that you pay the correct amount of taxes on time.

In the United States, the federal government, state governments, and some local governments impose taxes on individuals. These taxes are used to fund government programs and services, such as education, healthcare, and national defense. As a taxpayer, you play a vital role in supporting these programs and services by paying your taxes.

Your personal tax obligation depends on a variety of factors, including your income, your filing status, and the state and local taxes you are subject to. You may be eligible for deductions and credits that can reduce your tax liability, but you are still responsible for paying the taxes you owe.

To help you understand your personal tax obligation, you can use tax calculators and other tools to estimate your tax liability. You can also work with a tax professional to help you understand your tax obligations and ensure that you pay the correct amount of taxes. By understanding your personal tax obligation and paying your taxes on time, you can help support government programs and services and avoid penalties and other consequences.

Calculate Taxable Income

To calculate your taxable income, you will need to follow these steps:

Start with your gross income, which is the total amount of money you earn from all sources, including wages, salaries, tips, interest, dividends, and other income.

Subtract any adjustments to income, such as contributions to a traditional IRA or student loan interest, to arrive at your adjusted gross income.

Subtract any deductions you are eligible for, such as the standard deduction or itemized deductions, to arrive at your taxable income.

If you are eligible for any tax credits, such as the child tax credit or the earned income tax credit, you can subtract these credits from your taxable income to arrive at your final tax liability.

A Real Life Example

Here is an example of how to calculate taxable income using numbers and figures:

Start with your gross income, which is the total amount of money you earn from all sources. For this example, let's assume your gross income is $50,000.

Subtract any adjustments to income, such as contributions to a traditional IRA or student loan interest. Let's assume you have $1,000 in adjustments to income.

Subtract any deductions you are eligible for, such as the standard deduction or itemized deductions. Let's assume you are eligible for a standard deduction of $12,400.

If you are eligible for any tax credits, such as the child tax credit or the earned income tax credit, you can subtract these credits from your taxable income. Let's assume you are eligible for a child tax credit of $2,000.

Using these numbers, your taxable income would be calculated as follows:

Gross income: $50,000

Adjustments to income: -$1,000

Deductions: -$12,400

Taxable income: $36,600

Tax credits: -$2,000

Final tax liability: $34,600

In this example, your taxable income would be $36,600, and your final tax liability would be $34,600 after subtracting tax credits. You would need to pay taxes on this amount based on your tax bracket and other factors.

Evasion versus Avoidance

Tax evasion and tax avoidance are two different things. Tax evasion is the illegal practice of not paying taxes that are owed. It involves deliberately failing to report income, claiming false deductions, or hiding assets in order to reduce one's tax liability. Tax evasion is illegal and can result in penalties, fines, and even imprisonment.

Tax avoidance, on the other hand, is an opportunity. It is the legal practice of using tax laws and strategies to reduce one's tax liability. It involves taking advantage of deductions, credits, and other tax benefits that are available under the law in order to lower one's tax bill. Tax avoidance is legal, but it can sometimes be seen as unethical because it involves using the tax system to reduce one's tax liability.

In addition to the differences between tax evasion and tax avoidance, it is also important to understand the consequences of these two practices. Tax evasion is illegal and can result in severe penalties, while tax avoidance is legal but can sometimes be seen as unethical. It is important to understand the differences between these two practices and the consequences of each in order to make informed decisions about your own tax situation.

Personal tax obligation is an important aspect of financial planning. By understanding your tax obligations and paying your taxes on time, you can support government programs and services and avoid penalties and other consequences. By working with a tax professional, you can ensure that you are meeting your personal tax obligation and taking care of your financial health.

Chapter 8

The Financial Markets: Understanding How They Work

Different Types of Instruments

The overall financial market is a complex and dynamic system that involves various financial instruments and institutions. Here is an overview of some of the key elements of the financial market:

Stocks: A stock is a type of investment that represents ownership in a company. When you buy a stock, you are buying a share of the company's ownership, which entitles you to a share of the company's profits and voting rights. Stocks are traded on stock exchanges, such as the New York Stock Exchange (NYSE) or the NASDAQ, and can be bought and sold by investors.

Mutual funds: A mutual fund is a type of investment that pools money from many investors and invests it in a diversified portfolio of stocks, bonds, and other securities. Mutual funds are managed by professional investors, who use the pooled money to create a diversified portfolio that is designed to meet the fund's investment objective. Mutual funds can be bought and sold by investors, and their value is based on the value of the underlying securities in the fund's portfolio.

Bonds: A bond is a type of debt investment in which an investor loans money to a borrower, such as a corporation or government, in exchange for regular interest payments and the return of principal at maturity. Bonds are typically issued with a fixed interest rate and a specified maturity date, and can be traded on the bond market.

Derivatives: A derivative is a financial instrument that derives its value from an underlying asset, such as a stock, bond, commodity, or currency. Examples of derivatives include options, futures, and swaps. Derivatives are used to hedge risk, speculate on market movements, and provide liquidity in the financial market.

It is an important part of the economy, as it provides a way for companies and governments to raise capital, and for investors to earn a return on their investments.

How the market works?

Here is a simplified version of how the financial market works:

Companies and governments need capital to finance their operations and investments. They can raise capital by issuing stocks, bonds, and other securities.

Investors, such as individuals, institutions, and funds, are looking for ways to earn a return on their savings and investments. They can buy stocks, bonds, and other securities from companies and governments to earn a return on their investments.

The financial market is where stocks, bonds, and other securities are bought and sold. Stock exchanges, such as the NYSE or

NASDAQ, are marketplaces where stocks are traded. The bond market is where bonds are traded.

The price of stocks, bonds, and other securities is determined by supply and demand. If more investors want to buy a security than sell it, the price will go up. If more investors want to sell a security than buy it, the price will go down.

Financial institutions, such as banks and brokerage firms, play a key role in the financial market by providing services such as lending, trading, and investing. They facilitate the flow of capital between companies, governments, and investors.

Supply and Demand

Supply and demand is a fundamental concept in economics that explains how the price of a product or service is determined in the market. The same principles of supply and demand also apply to the financial market, where they play a crucial role in determining the price of stocks, bonds, and other securities. Here is a brief overview of how supply and demand works in the financial market:

The supply of a security in the financial market refers to the amount of the security that is available for sale. The supply of a security can be affected by various factors, such as the number of shares outstanding, the company's profitability, and the market conditions.

The demand for a security in the financial market refers to the amount of the security that investors are willing to buy. The demand for a security can be affected by various factors, such as the company's financial performance, the economic outlook, and the interest rates.

The price of a security in the financial market is determined by the interaction of supply and demand. If the supply of a security is greater than the demand for it, the price will tend to go down. If the demand for a security is greater than the supply of it, the price will tend to go up.

The supply and demand for a security in the financial market can change over time, depending on various factors. For example, if a company announces strong earnings, the demand for its stock may increase, which could push the stock price up. On the other hand, if the economic outlook deteriorates, the demand for stocks in general may decrease, which could cause stock prices to fall.

Supply and demand help determine the price of securities, and can change over time depending on various factors. Understanding how supply and demand works in the financial market can help investors make informed decisions about buying and selling securities.

The Players

here are various types of investors in the financial market, and each type of investor has its own unique characteristics and investment objectives. Some of the main types of investors include:

Individual investors: Individual investors are individuals who buy and sell stocks, bonds, and other securities for their own personal accounts. Individual investors may be motivated by various factors, such as the desire to earn a return on their savings, to grow their wealth, or to achieve financial independence.

Institutional investors: Institutional investors are large organizations, such as pension funds, insurance companies, and mutual funds, that invest on behalf of their clients. Institutional investors typically have a professional investment team and a large amount of capital to invest. They may be motivated by the desire to provide a stable return for their clients, to meet certain investment objectives, or to maximize their investment returns.

Retail investors: Retail investors are individual investors who buy and sell securities through a brokerage firm or online trading platform. Retail investors typically have a smaller amount of capital to invest compared to institutional investors. They may be motivated by the desire to earn a return on their savings, to grow their wealth, or to achieve financial independence.

Hedge funds: Hedge funds are private investment funds that use various investment strategies, such as leverage, short selling, and derivatives, to try to generate high returns. Hedge funds are typically only available to accredited investors, such as high-net-worth individuals or institutional investors. They may be motivated by the desire to earn high returns and outperform the market.

Understanding the financial market can help you make informed decisions about investing and managing your personal finances, and can provide insights into the broader economic environment.

Chapter 9

The Stock Market: Investing in Companies and Their Growth

Ownership of a Company

A stock market is a financial market where stocks, or shares of ownership in a company, are bought and sold. The stock market plays a crucial role in the economy by providing a way for companies to raise capital and for investors to earn a return on their investments.

Stocks are a type of investment that represents ownership in a company. When you buy a stock, you are buying a share of the company's ownership, which entitles you to a share of the company's profits and voting rights. For example, if you buy 100 shares of a company's stock, you own 100/1,000,000 = 0.01% of the company.

The stock market is where stocks are bought and sold. Stock exchanges, such as the NYSE and NASDAQ, are marketplaces where stocks are traded. The stock market is open to investors, who can buy and sell stocks through a brokerage firm or online trading platform. Investors can also use various investment strategies, such as diversification and asset allocation, to manage their stock portfolios.

The price of a stock is determined by supply and demand. If more investors want to buy a stock than sell it, the price will go up. If more investors want to sell a stock than buy it, the price will go down. The stock market is dynamic, and the price of a stock can change rapidly based on various factors, such as the company's financial performance, the economic outlook, and market conditions.

The stock market provides a way for companies to raise capital. When a company wants to raise money, it can issue new stocks, which can be bought by investors. This can provide the company with the capital it needs to finance its operations and investments. For example, if a company wants to expand its business, it can issue new stocks to raise the capital it needs to fund the expansion.

Misconceptions

There are many myths and misconceptions about the stock market, and it is important to understand the facts in order to make informed investment decisions. Here are a few myths about the stock market and the truth behind them:

Myth #1: The stock market always goes up: It is a common myth that the stock market always goes up over time, but this is not true. The stock market is subject to market forces, such as supply and demand, and the price of stocks can go up or down depending on various factors. In fact, the stock market has experienced many booms and busts throughout history, and it is important to understand the risks and potential rewards of investing in stocks.

Myth #2: You need a lot of money to invest in the stock market: It is a common myth that you need a lot of money to invest in the stock market, but this is not true. There are many investment options, such as mutual funds and exchange-traded funds, that allow investors to buy a diversified portfolio of stocks with a small amount of money. In addition, there are many online brokerage firms that offer low-cost trading options for individual investors.

Myth #3: You need to be an expert to invest in the stock market: It is a common myth that you need to be an expert to invest in the stock market, but this is not true. While it is important to educate yourself about investing and the stock market, there are many resources, such as financial advisors, investment guides, and online courses, that can help you learn the basics of investing. In addition, there are many investment options, such as index funds and ETFs, that provide a diversified portfolio of stocks and are managed by professional investors.

Types of Stocks

There are several different types of stocks, and each type has its own characteristics and risks. Here are a few of the main types of stocks:

Common stock: Common stock is the most common type of stock, and it represents ownership in a company. When you buy common stock, you are entitled to a share of the company's profits and voting rights. Common stock can provide investors with dividends, which are periodic payments from the company's profits, and capital gains, which are the profit from selling the stock at a higher price than you paid.

Preferred stock: Preferred stock is a type of stock that has a higher claim on the company's assets and earnings than common stock. When you buy preferred stock, you are entitled to a fixed dividend, which is a periodic payment from the company's profits, and you have priority over common stockholders if the company goes bankrupt. Preferred stock does not have voting rights, and it typically does not provide capital gains.

Blue-chip stock: Blue-chip stock is a type of stock that is issued by a well-established and financially stable company. Blue-chip companies are typically large and have a long track record of financial performance and dividends. Blue-chip stocks can provide investors with a steady stream of income and potential capital gains, but they also carry a higher level of risk than other types of stocks.

Penny stock: Penny stock is a type of stock that is issued by a small or micro-cap company, which is a company with a market capitalization of less than $300 million. Penny stocks are often considered to be risky investments, as they are not traded on major stock exchanges and are not subject to the same regulatory requirements as other stocks. Penny stocks can provide investors with high potential returns, but they also carry a high level of risk.

Beginner Steps in Trading a Stock

To trade a stock, you need to follow these steps:

Open a brokerage account: The first step to trading a stock is to open a brokerage account. A brokerage account is an account with a brokerage firm, such as Charles Schwab or Fidelity, that allows you to buy and sell stocks. To open a brokerage account, you need to provide personal information, such as your name, address, and Social Security number, and you may need to deposit money into your account to fund your trades.

Choose a stock: Once you have opened a brokerage account, you can choose a stock to trade. To choose a stock, you can research companies and their financial performance, read market news and analysis, and consult with a financial advisor. It is important to choose a stock that aligns with your investment objectives and risk tolerance.

Place an order: Once you have chosen a stock, you can place an order to buy or sell the stock. To place an order, you need to specify the stock you want to trade, the number of shares you want to buy or sell, and the price you are willing to pay or receive. There are various types of orders, such as market orders, limit orders, and stop-loss orders, that allow you to specify different conditions for your trade.

Execute the trade: Once your order is placed, the brokerage firm will try to execute the trade by finding a matching buyer or seller. If the trade is executed, the stock will be bought or sold at the agreed-upon price, and the shares will be added to or removed from your brokerage account. If the trade is not executed, your order will be canceled or remain open until it is filled.

Monitor your investment: Once you have bought or sold a stock, it is important to monitor your investment. This can help you understand how the stock is performing, identify potential risks and opportunities, and make decisions about buying or selling the stock. You can monitor your investment by checking the stock price, reading market news and analysis, and consulting with a financial advisor.

The stock market is an important part of the economy. It provides a way for companies to raise capital and for investors to earn a return on their investments. Understanding the stock market can help investors make informed decisions about buying and selling stocks.

Chapter 10

Mutual Funds: Investing in a Diversified Portfolio

A mutual fund is a type of investment vehicle that pools money from many investors and uses that money to buy a diversified portfolio of securities, such as stocks, bonds, and money market instruments. The value of a mutual fund is determined by the combined value of the securities it holds, and it is managed by a professional investment manager who seeks to generate returns for the investors in the fund.

One of the main advantages of investing in a mutual fund is diversification. Because a mutual fund invests in a wide range of securities, it is less risky than investing in a single stock or bond. This means that even if one of the securities in the fund's portfolio underperforms, the overall performance of the fund is less likely to be affected.

Another advantage of mutual funds is that they provide investors with professional management. The investment manager of a mutual fund is responsible for researching and selecting the securities that are included in the fund's portfolio. This can be beneficial for investors who don't have the time or expertise to manage their own investments.

Mutual funds are also highly liquid, meaning that investors can buy and sell shares in the fund at any time, subject to the fund's policies. This makes it easy for investors to access their money when they need it.

Mutual funds are sold by investment companies, and investors can choose from a wide range of funds that have different investment strategies and risk profiles. For example, some mutual funds may focus on a particular sector, such as technology or healthcare, while others may invest in a diverse range of companies across different industries. Some mutual funds may be more risky, with the potential for higher returns, while others may be more conservative, with a focus on preserving capital.

Breakdown of Various Funds

There are several different types of mutual funds, including:

Equity funds: These funds invest in stocks and aim to generate returns through capital appreciation. Within this category, there are sub-types such as large-cap funds, small-cap funds, and international funds.

Bond funds: These funds invest in bonds and aim to generate income through regular interest payments. Within this category, there are sub-types such as government bond funds, corporate bond funds, and high-yield bond funds.

Money market funds: These funds invest in short-term, low-risk instruments such as treasury bills and aim to provide a stable return with minimal volatility.

Balanced funds: These funds invest in a mix of stocks, bonds, and other securities, with the goal of achieving a balance of growth and income.

Specialty funds: These funds focus on a specific investment theme or sector, such as real estate, precious metals, or emerging markets.

Index funds: These funds aim to track the performance of a specific market index, such as the S&P 500 or the MSCI EAFE, by investing in the securities that make up the index.

Target-date funds: These funds are designed for investors with a specific retirement date in mind. The fund's asset allocation is automatically adjusted over time to become more conservative as the target date approaches.

Assess the Performances

There are several ways to access mutual fund performance, including:

Mutual fund prospectuses: Mutual fund companies are required to disclose the historical performance of their funds in the prospectus, which is a document that provides detailed information about the fund. Prospectuses are typically available on the mutual fund company's website or can be requested from the company.

If you want to learn about the performance of the XYZ Large Cap Fund, you could visit the XYZ Mutual Fund company's website and search for the fund's prospectus. The prospectus would provide information such as the fund's average annual return over the past 5 years, 10 years, and since inception.

Online databases: Websites such as Morningstar, Yahoo Finance, and Bloomberg provide historical performance data for a wide range of mutual funds. This data can be accessed for free or for a fee, depending on the website.

If you want to compare the performance of the XYZ Large Cap Fund to other large-cap funds, you could visit a website like Morningstar and search for the fund. The website would provide a performance chart showing the fund's return compared to its benchmark and peers.

Financial advisors: Financial advisors who offer mutual fund investment services can provide information about the performance of specific funds. Advisors may also be able to provide insight into the factors that have contributed to a fund's performance.

If you have a financial advisor who offers mutual fund investment services, you could ask them for information about the performance of the XYZ Large Cap Fund. The advisor may be able to provide additional context about the fund's performance, such as the sectors or companies that have contributed to its returns.

Building a Successful Mutual Fund Portfolio

Building a good mutual fund portfolio involves considering factors such as your investment goals, risk tolerance, time horizon, and diversification. Here are some steps to follow when building a mutual fund portfolio:

Determine your investment goals: What are you trying to achieve with your investments? Do you want to generate income, grow your wealth, or preserve your capital? Your investment goals will help guide your decisions about which mutual funds to include in your portfolio.

Assess your risk tolerance: How much risk are you willing to take with your investments? Are you comfortable with the potential for large swings in the value of your portfolio, or do you prefer a more stable investment approach? Your risk tolerance will help determine the mix of stocks, bonds, and other securities that you include in your portfolio.

Consider your time horizon: How long do you plan to invest your money? If you have a longer time horizon, you may be able to take on more risk in pursuit of higher returns. If you have a shorter time horizon, you may want to prioritize capital preservation over growth.

Diversify your portfolio: Diversification is a key principle of investing, and it involves spreading your money across a variety of assets and sectors to reduce your exposure to any single risk. When building a mutual fund portfolio, consider investing in a mix of equity funds, bond funds, and specialty funds to achieve diversification.

Monitor and rebalance your portfolio: As time goes on, the performance of your mutual funds and the overall allocation of your portfolio may change. It's important to regularly review your portfolio and make adjustments as needed to ensure that it continues to align with your investment goals and risk tolerance.

Building a good mutual fund portfolio requires careful planning and ongoing monitoring to ensure that it meets your needs and helps you achieve your investment objectives.

Chapter 11

The Bond Market: Investing in Debt Securities

Yes, you can buy Debts

The bond market is a financial market where investors can buy and sell bonds, which are debt instruments that pay a fixed or variable interest rate over a specific period of time. Bonds are issued by governments, municipalities, and corporations to raise capital for a variety of purposes, such as funding infrastructure projects, expanding businesses, or refinancing existing debt.

Investors in the bond market can earn income through the interest payments they receive on their bonds, and they can also potentially benefit from capital gains if they sell their bonds at a higher price than they paid for them. However, bond prices are also subject to changes in interest rates, which can impact the value of a bond and the return that an investor earns.

The bond market is an important source of financing for governments, municipalities, and corporations, and it also provides investors with an opportunity to diversify their portfolios and manage risk. The bond market is typically considered to be less risky than the stock market, but there are different types of bonds with varying levels of risk, so it's important for investors to carefully consider their investment options.

The Differences between Different Types of Bonds

There are several different types of bonds, including:

Government bonds: These bonds are issued by national governments to finance their operations and fund public projects. Government bonds are considered to be relatively safe investments because governments have the power to tax and borrow to make interest and principal payments.

Municipal bonds: These bonds are issued by cities, counties, and other local governments to finance public projects such as schools, hospitals, and roads. Municipal bonds are generally considered to be lower-risk investments than corporate bonds, but the creditworthiness of the issuing municipality can impact the risk of default.

Corporate bonds: These bonds are issued by companies to raise capital for a variety of purposes, such as expanding their operations or refinancing existing debt. Corporate bonds are generally considered to be riskier than government and municipal bonds because the issuer's ability to make interest and principal payments is dependent on its financial performance.

Treasury bonds: These bonds are issued by the U.S. government and are considered to be one of the safest investments because of the government's ability to make interest and principal payments. Treasury bonds have a long maturity, typically 10 to 30 years, and pay a fixed interest rate.

Treasury bills: These bonds are issued by the U.S. government and have a shorter maturity, typically 4 weeks to 1 year, and pay no interest. Instead, investors earn a return by purchasing the bonds at a discount to their face value and receiving the full face value when they mature.

High-yield bonds: These bonds, also known as junk bonds, are issued by companies that have a lower credit rating and are considered to be at higher risk of default. As a result, they pay a higher interest rate to compensate investors for the additional risk.

A Relatively Safer Bet

Bonds are often considered a safe haven because they tend to be less risky than other types of investments, such as stocks. This is because bonds are typically issued by governments and corporations, which have the ability to make regular interest and principal payments to bondholders. As a result, investors in bonds have a higher likelihood of receiving their principal and interest payments on time.

In addition, bonds are often seen as a defensive investment because they tend to perform well during times of economic uncertainty or market volatility. This is because investors may flock to bonds as a safe haven, driving up bond prices and reducing yields. As a result, bonds can provide a degree of stability and income for investors who are concerned about the potential risks in the stock market.

Of course, it's important to note that not all bonds are equally safe. The creditworthiness of the issuer, the type of bond, and the bond's terms and conditions can all impact the risk of default and the potential return for the investor. However, on average, bonds are considered to be a relatively safe investment option compared to stocks and other securities.

Chapter 12

Diversification: The Key to Long-Term Investing Success

Eggs in Different Baskets

Diversification is a key principle of investing that involves spreading your money across a variety of assets and sectors to reduce your exposure to any single risk. The idea is that by investing in a diverse range of assets, you can protect your portfolio from the potential impact of market volatility or economic downturns.

For example, if you have a portfolio that is heavily weighted towards a single stock or sector, you are exposed to the risk that the performance of that stock or sector will decline. However, if you diversify your portfolio by including stocks from different sectors, bonds, and other assets, you can reduce the impact of any single stock or sector on your overall portfolio performance.

Diversification can also help you manage risk by allowing you to tailor your portfolio to your specific investment goals and risk tolerance. For example, if you are a conservative investor who is focused on capital preservation, you may want to include a higher proportion of bonds in your portfolio to reduce volatility. On the other hand, if you are a growth-oriented investor, you may want to include a higher proportion of stocks in your portfolio to take advantage of potential upside.

The Weight of Different Assets

The ideal allocation of stocks, bonds, and other assets in your investment portfolio will depend on your specific investment goals, risk tolerance, and time horizon. There is no one-size-fits-all answer to the question of how much to put in stocks and how much in bonds, as it will vary depending on your individual circumstances.

Generally speaking, however, investors who are younger and have a longer time horizon may be able to take on more risk and allocate a higher proportion of their portfolio to stocks. This is because stocks have the potential for higher returns over the long term, but they are also more volatile and subject to market fluctuations.

Conversely, investors who are older and have a shorter time horizon may want to allocate a higher proportion of their portfolio to bonds. This is because bonds are generally considered to be less risky than stocks and can provide a stable source of income. However, it's important to keep in mind that bond prices are also subject to changes in interest rates, which can impact the value of your bonds and the return you earn on them.

Ultimately, the right allocation of stocks, bonds, and other assets in your portfolio will depend on your individual investment objectives, risk tolerance, and financial situation.

The Metrics to Access a Diversified Portfolio

There are several formulas and metrics that investors can use to assess the performance of a diversified portfolio, including:

Return on investment (ROI): This is a measure of the profit or loss on an investment, expressed as a percentage of the investment's cost. To calculate ROI, you divide the net gain or loss on the investment by the investment's cost and multiply by 100. For example, if you invest $100 and earn a net return of $20, your ROI would be 20%.

Sharpe ratio: This is a measure of the risk-adjusted return of an investment, which takes into account the investment's volatility. To calculate the Sharpe ratio, you divide the investment's excess return (i.e. the return above the risk-free rate) by its standard deviation. A higher Sharpe ratio indicates that the investment has generated a higher return for the amount of risk taken.

Alpha: This is a measure of the excess return of an investment relative to its benchmark. To calculate alpha, you subtract the investment's benchmark return from its actual return. A positive alpha indicates that the investment has outperformed its benchmark, while a negative alpha indicates that it has underperformed.

Beta: This is a measure of the volatility of an investment relative to its benchmark. To calculate beta, you divide the investment's volatility by the volatility of its benchmark. A beta of 1 indicates that the investment has the same volatility as its benchmark, while a beta greater than 1 indicates that it is more volatile, and a beta less than 1 indicates that it is less volatile.

Overall, these formulas and metrics can provide insight into the performance of a diversified portfolio and help investors assess the effectiveness of their investment strategy. However, it's important to keep in mind that these metrics are not the only factors to consider when evaluating the performance of a portfolio, and they should be used in combination with other factors such as the portfolio's overall risk and return profile.

Diversification is an important tool for investors who want to manage risk and maximize the potential return on their investments. By spreading their money across a range of assets, investors can reduce the impact of market volatility and achieve a more balanced and well-rounded investment portfolio.

Chapter 13

Risk and Reward: Understanding the Trade-Offs of Investing

Risk versus Reward

Risk and reward are two important concepts in investment that are closely related. In general, the risk of an investment refers to the potential for loss of principal or the chance that the investment will not perform as expected. The reward of an investment, on the other hand, refers to the potential return or profit that an investor can expect to earn on the investment.

In general, there is a trade-off between risk and reward in investment. This means that investments with higher potential returns typically have higher levels of risk, while investments with lower potential returns have lower levels of risk. For example, stocks are generally considered to be riskier than bonds because they have the potential for higher returns but also higher volatility.

When making investment decisions, it's important for investors to consider both the potential risk and the potential reward of an investment. By understanding the level of risk that an investment carries, investors can make informed decisions about whether the potential reward is worth the potential risk.

Not a Straightforward Relationship

The relationship between risk and reward in investment is not always straightforward, and there are many factors that can impact the potential return on an investment. As a result, it's not always true that high risk investments will provide higher rewards, and there are many cases where investments with high levels of risk may not deliver the expected return.

One reason why high risk does not always mean higher reward is that the performance of an investment is not solely determined by its level of risk. Other factors, such as the quality of the investment, the performance of the underlying assets, and changes in market conditions, can also impact the return on an investment. For example, an investment may have a high level of risk but underperform due to poor market conditions or the performance of the underlying assets.

Additionally, the relationship between risk and reward can vary depending on the time horizon of the investment. Over the long term, investments with higher levels of risk may have a higher potential for growth and provide higher returns. However, over the short term, these same investments may be more volatile and subject to larger swings in value. As a result, the potential reward of a high-risk investment may not be realized in the short term, despite its long-term potential.

Overall, while there is a general relationship between risk and reward in investment, it's important to remember that there are many factors that can impact the potential return on an investment. As a result, high risk does not always mean higher reward, and investors should carefully evaluate the risks and rewards of each investment in their portfolio to make informed decisions about their investments.

Chapter 14

Financial Advisors: How They Can Help You Achieve Your Goals

Financial advisors are professional advisors who provide guidance and advice to individuals and businesses on financial matters. Financial advisors are typically trained and licensed to provide financial planning and investment advice, and they can help clients with a range of financial issues, including retirement planning, asset allocation, estate planning, and tax planning.

Financial advisors may work for financial planning firms, brokerage firms, or banks, or they may be independent advisors who work on a freelance basis. Financial advisors typically have a background in finance, economics, or a related field, and they may hold professional designations such as the Certified Financial Planner (CFP) or Chartered Financial Analyst (CFA) designation.

The role of a financial advisor is to provide expert advice and guidance to clients on financial matters, based on their individual goals, risk tolerance, and financial situation. Financial advisors can help clients develop a personalized financial plan that meets their unique needs, and they can also provide ongoing support and advice to help clients implement and maintain their financial plan.

Who are they really?

There are several different types of financial advisors, each with a different focus and area of expertise. Some common types of financial advisors include:

Financial planners: Financial planners provide comprehensive financial planning and advice to clients, including retirement planning, estate planning, tax planning, and risk management. Financial planners may be generalists who provide advice on a range of financial topics, or they may specialize in a specific area, such as retirement planning or estate planning.

Wealth managers: Wealth managers provide investment advice and portfolio management services to high-net-worth individuals and families. Wealth managers typically have a deep understanding of investment strategies and can help clients develop a personalized investment plan that aligns with their goals and risk tolerance.

Retirement advisors: Retirement advisors specialize in providing advice and guidance on retirement planning, including helping clients save for retirement, invest their retirement savings, and develop a plan for distributing their assets in retirement. Retirement advisors may work with clients of all ages, from those who are just starting to save for retirement to those who are already in retirement.

Insurance advisors: Insurance advisors provide advice and guidance on insurance products, including life insurance, health insurance, and disability insurance. Insurance advisors can help clients understand the different types of insurance and how they can be used to protect against financial loss and provide for their families in the event of death or illness.

Engage an Expert

It's important to engage a financial advisor for several reasons. First, financial advisors are trained and licensed to provide expert advice and guidance on financial matters, and they can help clients understand complex financial concepts and strategies. By working with a financial advisor, clients can gain access to professional expertise and knowledge that they may not have on their own.

Second, financial advisors can help clients develop a personalized financial plan that meets their unique needs and goals. Financial advisors can provide objective advice and guidance, taking into account the client's individual financial situation, risk tolerance, and goals. This can help clients make informed decisions about their money and achieve their financial objectives.

Third, financial advisors can provide ongoing support and guidance to help clients implement and maintain their financial plan. Financial advisors can help clients stay on track with their financial goals, monitor their investments, and make adjustments to their plan as needed. This can help clients stay on top of their financial situation and make progress towards achieving their financial goals.

Overall, engaging a financial advisor can provide many benefits to clients, including access to professional expertise, personalized financial planning, and ongoing support and guidance. By working with a financial advisor, clients can gain a better understanding of their financial situation and take control of their financial future.

Chapter 15

The Real Estate Game: Investing in Property

Your Property

Real estate refers to land and any buildings or structures on that land. Real estate can be residential, commercial, or industrial, and it can include a wide range of property types, such as single-family homes, apartments, office buildings, shopping centers, and factories.

Real estate can be owned by individuals, businesses, or governments, and it can be used for a variety of purposes, such as living, working, or investing. The value of real estate is determined by a variety of factors, including location, size, condition, and demand.

Real estate can be bought and sold through real estate agents or brokers, and it can also be leased to tenants. Many people invest in real estate as a way to build wealth and generate income, either by buying and holding properties or by buying and flipping properties for a profit.

Your Mortgage

A mortgage is a type of loan that is used to finance the purchase of real estate. When you take out a mortgage, you borrow money from a lender to pay for the property, and you agree to repay the loan over a period of time, usually 15 or 30 years.

To secure the loan, the lender requires you to put up the property as collateral, which means that if you fail to make the required payments, the lender can take ownership of the property. The terms of a mortgage loan, including the interest rate, loan term, and monthly payments, are typically determined based on the borrower's credit history, income, and debt-to-income ratio.

When you take out a mortgage, you are required to make regular monthly payments to the lender, which typically include both interest and principal. The interest portion of the payment goes to the lender as compensation for providing the loan, while the principal portion goes towards paying down the loan balance. Over time, as you make regular payments, the loan balance decreases and you build equity in the property.

Calculating Mortgage Loan – An Example

To calculate a mortgage loan, you need to know the following information:

The loan amount: This is the amount you want to borrow from the lender to finance the purchase of the property. For example, if the property you want to buy is $500,000, you may want to take out a loan for $400,000 to cover the purchase price and closing costs.

The interest rate: This is the annual interest rate that the lender will charge you for the loan. The interest rate can vary depending on a variety of factors, including the lender, your credit score, and market conditions. For example, if the interest rate on your loan is

3.75%, the lender will charge you 3.75% interest on the outstanding loan balance each year.

The loan term: This is the length of time you have to repay the loan. Most mortgage loans have a term of 15 or 30 years, but some lenders may offer shorter or longer terms. For example, if the loan term is 30 years, you will have 30 years to repay the loan, with regular monthly payments.

To calculate the monthly mortgage payment, you can use the following formula:

Monthly mortgage payment = (Loan amount x Interest rate) / (1 - (1 + Interest rate)^(-Loan term))

For example, if you want to borrow $400,000 at a 3.75% interest rate for 30 years, your monthly mortgage payment would be:

Monthly mortgage payment = ($400,000 x 0.0375) / (1 - (1 + 0.0375)^(-30))

Monthly mortgage payment = $1,822.03

In this example, your monthly mortgage payment would be $1,822.03, which includes both interest and principal. Over the course of the loan term, your monthly payments would gradually reduce the loan balance and build equity in the property.

In addition to the monthly mortgage payment, you may also be required to pay other costs and fees associated with the loan, such as closing costs, property taxes, and insurance. These costs can vary depending on the lender and the terms of the loan, and it's important to understand all of the costs and fees associated with the loan before you agree to the terms.

Buying Property is NOT always a Win

A property's value can appreciate over time for a variety of reasons. Some common factors that can contribute to property appreciation include:

Location: Properties in desirable locations, such as near good schools, parks, or public transportation, tend to appreciate in value over time. This is because people are willing to pay a premium for the convenience and amenities that these locations offer.

Economic growth: As the economy grows and more people move into an area, demand for housing typically increases, which can lead to property appreciation. For example, if a new employer moves into an area and creates many new jobs, more people may move into the area, which can drive up demand for housing and lead to property appreciation.

Renovations and improvements: If a property is well-maintained and has been updated with modern features and amenities, it can appreciate in value over time. For example, if you add a new bathroom or kitchen to a property, it can make the property more desirable and increase its value.

On the other hand, there are also several factors that can cause a property's value to decrease or remain stable over time. Some common reasons why a property may not appreciate in value include:

Economic downturns: Economic downturns can lead to reduced demand for housing and decreased property values. For example, if there is a recession and many people lose their jobs, they may be unable to afford to buy a home, which can lead to a decrease in property values.

Neighborhood decline: If a neighborhood experiences decline, it can impact the value of the properties in that area. For example, if crime rates increase or the quality of local schools decreases, people may be less willing to buy homes in the area, which can lead to decreased property values.

Physical condition: The physical condition of a property can also impact its value. If a property is in poor condition and requires significant repairs, it may be less desirable to potential buyers, which can lead to decreased property values.

Real estate is a valuable asset class that can provide a wide range of benefits to individuals, businesses, and communities. By understanding the fundamentals of real estate, investors can make informed decisions about buying, selling, and investing in real estate.

Chapter 16

Precious Metals: Investing in Gold and Other Commodities

Precious metals investment refers to the purchase and ownership of precious metals, such as gold, silver, platinum, and palladium, for the purpose of generating a return on the investment. Precious metals are often considered a "safe haven" investment because they can hold their value during times of economic uncertainty or market volatility.

Precious metals can be bought and sold in a variety of forms, including coins, bars, and rounds. Investors can also invest in precious metals indirectly through exchange-traded funds (ETFs) or mutual funds that hold precious metals as part of their portfolio.

Precious metals investments can provide several potential benefits to investors. Because precious metals are physical assets, they can provide a hedge against inflation and currency devaluation. They can also provide diversification to an investment portfolio, reducing the overall risk and volatility of the portfolio.

However, there are also risks associated with precious metals investment. The value of precious metals can fluctuate based on a variety of factors, including supply and demand, market conditions, and geopolitical events. Additionally, precious metals can be difficult to value and they may not generate a regular income like stocks or bonds.

A Difficult Choice

The decision to invest in precious metals compared to stocks and bonds is a personal one that depends on an individual's investment objectives and risk tolerance. Precious metals can provide diversification and protection against inflation, and they can also offer the potential for capital appreciation. However, they can also be volatile and do not generate a regular income like stocks and bonds.

For investors who are looking to diversify their portfolio and protect against inflation, precious metals can be a valuable addition to their investment mix. By holding a mix of stocks, bonds, and precious metals, investors can spread their risk across different asset classes and reduce the impact of market volatility on their portfolio.

However, it's important to remember that the value of precious metals can be volatile, and that they do not generate a regular income like stocks and bonds. This means that investors who are looking for regular income from their investments may not find precious metals to be an appealing option. Additionally, the costs and challenges associated with buying, storing, and valuing physical precious metals can make them a less appealing option for some investors.

The decision to invest in precious metals compared to stocks and bonds is a personal one that depends on an individual's investment objectives and risk tolerance. By understanding the potential benefits and drawbacks of precious metals investment, investors can make informed decisions about whether they want to include precious metals in their investment portfolio.

Chapter 17

Cryptocurrency: The Future of Money?

Cryptocurrency is a digital or virtual currency that uses cryptography for security and is decentralized, meaning it is not controlled by a central authority like a bank or government. Cryptocurrency is often used as a medium of exchange for goods and services, and it can be traded on online exchanges for fiat currency or other cryptocurrencies.

Cryptocurrency is based on blockchain technology, which is a distributed ledger that records transactions on multiple computers, making it transparent and secure. The first and most well-known cryptocurrency is Bitcoin, which was created in 2009. Since then, thousands of other cryptocurrencies have been created, with varying features and uses.

Cryptocurrency has gained popularity in recent years as a way to make online payments, store value, and transfer money without the need for a central authority. However, it is also highly volatile and is not backed by any physical

Why it may or may not be the future

There are several reasons why cryptocurrency may be the future of money, including:

Decentralization: Cryptocurrency is decentralized, meaning it is not controlled by a central authority like a bank or government. This makes it transparent, secure, and immune to censorship or interference by external parties. This could make it a more efficient and equitable way of conducting transactions compared to traditional forms of money.

Speed and low transaction costs: Cryptocurrency transactions are fast and can be processed 24/7. They also often have low transaction fees, which can make them an attractive option for making online payments or transferring money internationally. This could make cryptocurrency a more efficient and affordable way of conducting transactions compared to traditional forms of money.

Innovation: Cryptocurrency and blockchain technology are still relatively new, and there is a lot of potential for innovation in this space. For example, smart contract technology, which allows for the automatic execution of agreements, could enable new and more efficient ways of conducting transactions and transferring value. This could make cryptocurrency a more innovative and dynamic way of conducting transactions compared to traditional forms of money.

On the other hand, there are also several reasons why cryptocurrency may not be the future of money. Some potential drawbacks of cryptocurrency include:

Volatility: Cryptocurrency is highly volatile, and its value can fluctuate dramatically based on a variety of factors, including supply and demand, market conditions, and regulatory developments. This volatility can make it difficult for people to use cryptocurrency as a stable store of value or medium of exchange, and it can also lead to losses for investors.

Lack of widespread acceptance: Cryptocurrency is not widely accepted as a form of payment, and many merchants and businesses do not accept it as a valid form of payment. This can make it difficult for people to use cryptocurrency in their daily lives, and it can limit its potential as a medium of exchange.

Regulation: Cryptocurrency is not regulated in the same way as traditional forms of money, and there is uncertainty about how it will be regulated in the future. This lack of regulatory oversight can create risks for investors, and it can also create challenges for governments and central banks in terms of monetary policy and financial stability.

Easy Steps to get into the Crypto World

There are a few easy steps you can follow to buy cryptocurrency:

Choose a cryptocurrency exchange: Cryptocurrency is traded on online exchanges, and there are many different exchanges to choose from. It's important to research and compare the different exchanges to find one that suits your needs, such as one that offers a wide range of cryptocurrencies, low fees, and a user-friendly interface.

Create an account: Once you've chosen an exchange, you'll need to create an account by providing some personal information and verifying your identity. This is usually done through email or SMS verification.

Deposit funds: Once your account is set up, you'll need to deposit funds into your account in order to buy cryptocurrency. Most exchanges accept fiat currency, such as USD or EUR, and you can usually deposit funds through a bank transfer or credit card.

Buy cryptocurrency: Once you have funds in your account, you can buy cryptocurrency by placing an order on the exchange. You'll need to specify the amount of cryptocurrency you want to buy, and the exchange will match your order with other buyers or sellers on the platform.

Store your cryptocurrency: After you've bought cryptocurrency, it's important to store it securely. Most exchanges offer a wallet service where you can store your cryptocurrency, but this is not always the most secure option. It's often recommended to store your cryptocurrency in a hardware wallet, which is a physical device that allows you to securely store your cryptocurrency offline.

Hackers' Heaven

Cryptocurrency can be hacked easily because it is stored and managed on digital platforms, which are vulnerable to cyber attacks. Hackers can use a variety of methods to gain access to cryptocurrency, such as phishing scams, malware, and vulnerabilities in the underlying blockchain technology.

One of the main ways to avoid being hacked when using cryptocurrency is to use a hardware wallet. A hardware wallet is a physical device that allows you to store your cryptocurrency offline, providing an extra layer of security. By storing your cryptocurrency in a hardware wallet, you can avoid having it hacked from your computer or phone.

Another way to avoid being hacked when using cryptocurrency is to be cautious and vigilant. This means not sharing your private keys or other sensitive information with anyone, avoiding suspicious websites and emails, and keeping your software and security protocols up to date.

Overall, cryptocurrency can be vulnerable to hacking because it is stored and managed on digital platforms. To avoid being hacked, it's important to use a hardware wallet and to be cautious and vigilant when using cryptocurrency.

Chapter 18

The Power of Compound Interest: Understanding Retirement Accounts

Compound interest is the interest that is earned on the initial principal and on the accumulated interest of a deposit or loan. It is called "compound" interest because the interest is calculated on the principal plus any accumulated interest.

Compound interest can be a powerful tool for growing wealth, because it allows interest to be earned on interest. However, it can also work against you if you are borrowing money, because the interest will be added to your principal and will continue to accrue, increasing the total amount you owe.

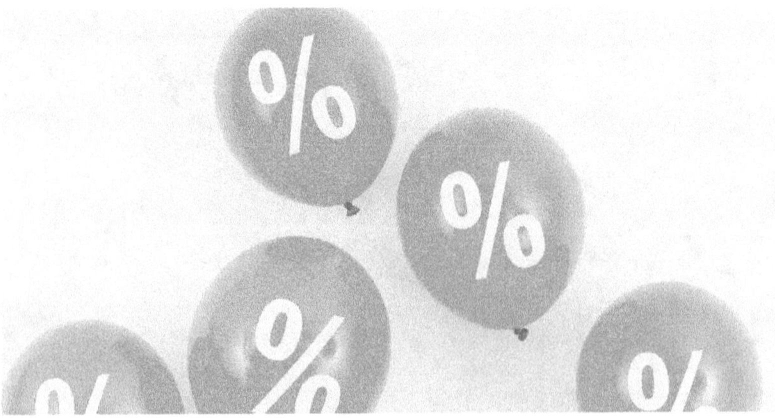

Interest on Interest

Imagine you deposit $1,000 in a savings account that pays 5% interest per year, compounded annually. Here's how your balance would grow over time:

After the first year, you would earn 5% interest on your $1,000 deposit, which is $50. Your total balance would be $1,050.

After the second year, you would earn 5% interest on your $1,050 balance, which is $52.50. Your total balance would be $1,102.50.

After the third year, you would earn 5% interest on your $1,102.50 balance, which is $55.13. Your total balance would be $1,157.63.

As you can see, each year your interest is calculated on the principal plus the accumulated interest, so your balance grows more and more each year.

Now, let's imagine that you withdraw the interest each year instead of leaving it in the account. Here's how your balance would grow over time:

After the first year, you would earn 5% interest on your $1,000 deposit, which is $50. Your total balance would be $1,000, but you would have withdrawn the $50 in interest, so your ending balance would be the same as your starting balance.

After the second year, you would earn 5% interest on your $1,000 deposit, which is $50. Your total balance would be $1,050, but you would have withdrawn the $50 in interest, so your ending balance would be the same as your starting balance.

After the third year, you would earn 5% interest on your $1,000 deposit, which is $50. Your total balance would be $1,100, but you would have withdrawn the $50 in interest, so your ending balance would be the same as your starting balance.

As you can see, by withdrawing the interest each year, you don't benefit from compound interest, and your balance stays the same over time.

Compound interest is the interest that is earned on the initial principal and on the accumulated interest of a deposit or loan. It can be a powerful tool for growing wealth, but it can also work against you if you are borrowing money.

Chapter 19

Inflation: Understanding Its Impact on Your Money

Inflation is a measure of how much the prices of goods and services have increased over a period of time. It is typically measured as an annual percentage increase, and is calculated by taking the current price of a good or service, dividing it by the price of the same good or service in the previous period, and then multiplying by 100. For example, if the price of a loaf of bread was $3.00 last year and it is $3.25 this year, the inflation rate for bread would be: (3.25/3.00) * 100 = 108.33. This means that the price of bread has increased by 8.33% over the past year.

Inflation can have a number of negative effects on the economy. For one, it can reduce the purchasing power of consumers, because their money is worth less over time. Inflation can also lead to higher interest rates, as lenders try to compensate for the fact that their money will be worth less in the future. This can make borrowing more expensive, and can slow down economic growth.

Monetary Policy

Monetary policy is the process by which a central bank, such as the Federal Reserve in the United States, manages the supply of money in the economy. This is done in order to achieve certain goals, such as low unemployment and stable prices.

One way that monetary policy can be used to control inflation is by raising interest rates. When interest rates are high, it becomes more expensive for people and businesses to borrow money, which can slow down spending and economic growth. As a result, the demand for goods and services may decrease, and this can help to keep prices from rising too quickly.

Another way that monetary policy can be used to control inflation is by changing the money supply. Central banks can use a variety of tools, such as open market operations, to increase or decrease the amount of money in circulation. If the money supply is increased, this can lead to more spending and economic growth, but it can also cause prices to rise. If the money supply is decreased, this can help to reduce inflation by slowing down spending and economic growth.

In general, the goal of monetary policy is to achieve a low, stable rate of inflation that is consistent with healthy economic growth.

Fiscal Policy

Fiscal policy is the process by which governments use their spending and taxing powers to influence the economy. This is different from monetary policy.

One way that fiscal policy can be used to control inflation is by increasing taxes. When taxes are high, people and businesses have less money to spend, which can help to reduce demand for goods and services. This can help to keep prices from rising too quickly.

Another way that fiscal policy can be used to control inflation is by reducing government spending. When the government spends less money, this can help to slow down the economy and reduce demand for goods and services. This can also help to keep prices from rising too quickly.

Governments use a variety of tools and techniques to achieve this goal, and they must carefully balance the need to control inflation with the need to support economic growth.

Holding too much cash is generally a bad idea

Holding cash is generally considered to be a bad idea because of inflation. This is because the value of cash tends to decrease over time as prices for goods and services rise. For example, if the inflation rate is 2% per year, the purchasing power of a dollar today will be worth about 98 cents one year from now. This means that if you have $100 in cash today, it will only be worth about $98 in a year from time, even if you don't spend it.

In addition to losing purchasing power over time, holding cash can also be risky in other ways. Cash can be lost or stolen, and it doesn't earn any interest, so it won't help you to build wealth.

In general, it is better to invest your money in assets that are likely to increase in value, such as stocks, bonds, or real estate. These assets can help you to protect your wealth from the effects of inflation, and they can also help you to earn a return on your investment.

Chapter 20

Emergency Funds: Protecting Yourself from Financial Shock

An emergency fund is a set amount of money that is set aside to be used in case of an unexpected financial event, such as a job loss, illness, or natural disaster. Emergency funds are important because they can help to provide financial stability and security in times of need.

The amount of money that should be kept in an emergency fund can vary depending on individual circumstances, but a general rule of thumb is to have enough money saved to cover at least three to six months' worth of expenses. This will ensure that you have enough money to cover your basic needs, such as food, housing, and transportation, if you are unable to earn an income for an extended period of time.

Emergency funds should be kept in a safe and easily accessible place, such as a savings account or a money market fund. They should also be separate from your regular savings and investment accounts, so that they are not accidentally spent on non-emergency expenses.

Having an emergency fund can provide peace of mind and financial security in case of unexpected events. It is an important part of a healthy financial plan, and can help you to weather any financial storms that may come your way.

How much is enough?

The amount of money that should be kept in an emergency fund can vary depending on individual circumstances, but a general rule of thumb is to have enough money saved to cover at least three to six months' worth of expenses. This will ensure that you have enough money to cover your basic needs, such as food, housing, and transportation, if you are unable to earn an income for an extended period of time.

The exact amount of money that you should have in your emergency fund will depend on factors such as your income, expenses, and the stability of your job. For example, if you have a high-paying job with a stable income and few expenses, you may be able to get by with a smaller emergency fund. On the other hand, if you have a lower-paying job with a fluctuating income and many expenses, you may need to have a larger emergency fund to protect yourself in case of a financial emergency.

It is a good idea to review your emergency fund on a regular basis, and make sure that it is adequately funded to cover your needs. This will help you to be prepared for any unexpected financial events that may arise, and will provide peace of mind and financial security.

Chapter 21

Planning for Your Golden Years: Retirement Strategies

Retirement planning is the process of preparing for your retirement, which is the period of your life when you will no longer be working and earning an income. Retirement planning involves a number of different steps, including estimating how much money you will need to save in order to live comfortably during your retirement, choosing the right types of investment and savings vehicles to help you reach your goals, and developing a plan for how you will spend your time during retirement.

One important aspect of retirement planning is estimating how much money you will need to save. This will depend on factors such as your expected retirement age, your desired standard of living, and the amount of money you will be receiving from sources such as Social Security and pension plans. You will also need to consider how long you will be retired, and how your expenses may change over time.

Another important aspect of retirement planning is choosing the right types of investment and savings vehicles. This will depend on your individual circumstances, such as your risk tolerance, your time horizon, and your current financial situation. Some common options for retirement savings include 401(k) plans, Individual Retirement Accounts (IRAs), and employer-sponsored pension plans.

Framework for Retirement Planning

To plan for retirement, there are a few key steps you can follow:

Estimate how much money you will need to save: The first step in retirement planning is to estimate how much money you will need to save in order to live comfortably during your retirement. This will depend on factors such as your expected retirement age, your desired standard of living, and the amount of money you will be receiving from sources such as Social Security and pension plans.

Choose the right types of investment and savings vehicles: Once you have a target savings amount, you will need to choose the right investment and savings vehicles to help you reach your goals. This will depend on your individual circumstances, such as your risk tolerance, your time horizon, and your current financial situation. Some common options for retirement savings include 401(k) plans, Individual Retirement Accounts (IRAs), and employer-sponsored pension plans.

Develop a plan for how you will spend your time during retirement: Retirement is not just about money - it is also about how you will spend your time. Developing a plan for how you will spend your time during retirement can help to ensure that you have a fulfilling and enjoyable retirement. This may involve activities such as traveling, pursuing hobbies, volunteering, or spending time with family and friends.

Review your plan regularly: Finally, it is important to review your retirement plan on a regular basis, and make any necessary adjustments. This will ensure that your plan remains on track, and that it continues to meet your changing needs and goals.

Retirement planning is an important part of your financial plan, and it is never too early to start. By taking the time to develop a plan and save for your retirement, you can ensure that you will have the financial resources you need to live comfortably and enjoy your golden years.

Chapter 22

Financial Legacy: How to Leave a Positive Impact on Future Generations

Leaving wealth to your future generation can be an important way to provide financial security and stability for your loved ones. It can also be a way to pass on your values and legacy, and to help your descendants to achieve their own goals and dreams.

There are a few key reasons why leaving wealth to your future generation can be important:

Financial security: One of the main reasons to leave wealth to your future generation is to provide financial security and stability for your loved ones. By leaving them a financial inheritance, you can help them to pay for education, buy a home, start a business, or pursue other financial goals.

Passing on your values and legacy: Leaving wealth to your future generation can also be a way to pass on your values and legacy. You can use your inheritance to help your descendants to live according to the principles and beliefs that are important to you, and to support causes and organizations that you care about.

Supporting your descendants' goals and dreams: Finally, leaving wealth to your future generation can be a way to support your descendants' goals and dreams. Whether they want to travel the world, start a family, or pursue a career in a particular field, your inheritance can provide the financial resources they need to achieve their goals.

A Will – A Legal Document

A will is a legal document that outlines how you want your property and assets to be distributed after you die. Having a will is important because it allows you to have control over what happens to your property and assets, and to make sure that they are distributed according to your wishes.

There are a few key reasons why having a will is important:

Ensuring that your property and assets are distributed according to your wishes: One of the main reasons to have a will is to make sure that your property and assets are distributed according to your wishes. Without a will, the laws of your state will determine how your property and assets are distributed, which may not be in line with your wishes.

Avoiding disputes and conflicts among your heirs: Another important reason to have a will is to avoid disputes and conflicts among your heirs. By clearly outlining how you want your property and assets to be distributed, you can help to prevent disagreements and legal battles among your loved ones.

Making it easier for your loved ones to settle your estate: Finally, having a will can make it easier for your loved ones to settle your estate. Your will can provide clear instructions on how to distribute your property and assets, and it can also name an executor who will be responsible for carrying out your wishes. This can help to make the process of settling your estate smoother and less stressful for your loved ones.

Overall, leaving wealth to your future generation can be an important way to provide financial security, pass on your values and legacy, and support your descendants' goals and dreams. By planning ahead, you can ensure that your wealth will continue to make a positive impact on the lives of your loved ones for generations to come.

Empowering Yourself with Financial Freedom

As you have read through the pages of "The Financial Foundations: Building a Strong Personal Economy," you have been introduced to the fundamental principles of personal finance. From understanding the basics of money management to learning about the complexities of investing in the stock market, this book has provided you with a wealth of valuable knowledge and insights.

With this knowledge, you are now equipped to take control of your financial future and build the life you want. Whether you are just starting out on your financial journey or you are a seasoned pro, the principles and strategies outlined in this book can help you achieve your goals and achieve financial freedom.

I encourage you to continue learning and growing as you strive towards your financial goals. As you do, remember that the power of financial knowledge is a powerful tool that can empower you to make informed decisions and achieve success.

Congratulations on completing "The Financial Foundations" and best of luck on your financial journey.

A Favor

Thank you for reading, I hope you can leave a few kind words.

Your review will motivate us to do better.

Tom Y. Baker

Dropped Out Traders (DOT)

All Our Books

Follow me to stay up-to-date with my new books!

www.ingramcontent.com/pod-product-compliance
Lightning Source LLC
LaVergne TN
LVHW022059200926
848481LV00003B/984